T0417788

URSA

THE WORLD OF PHYSICS

SPACE & TIME

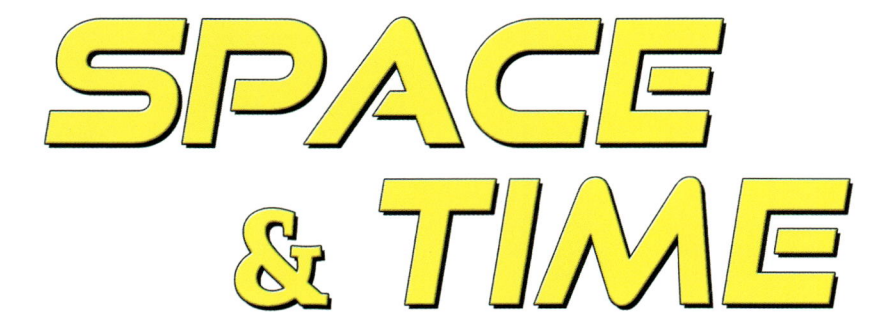

by
Tom Jackson

BEARPORT
PUBLISHING

Minneapolis, Minnesota

Bearport Publishing Company Product Development Team

Publisher: Jen Jenson; Director of Product Development: Spencer Brinker; Managing Editor: Allison Juda; Editor: Cole Nelson; Associate Editor: Naomi Reich; Associate Editor: Tiana Tran; Art Director: Colin O'Dea; Designer: Kim Jones; Designer: Kayla Eggert; Product Development Specialist: Owen Hamlin

Statement on Usage of Generative Artificial Intelligence

Bearport Publishing remains committed to publishing high-quality nonfiction books. Therefore, we restrict the use of generative AI to ensure accuracy of all text and visual components pertaining to a book's subject. See BearportPublishing.com for details.

Library of Congress Cataloging-in-Publication Data is available at www.loc.gov or upon request from the publisher.

ISBN: 979-8-89232-897-5 (hardcover)
ISBN: 979-8-89232-927-9 (ebook)

For more information, write to Bearport Publishing, 5357 Penn Avenue South, Minneapolis, MN 55419.

Contents

A Mysterious Universe

Since the earliest humans started watching the stars, space and time have been the source of many scientific mysteries. Even with powerful telescopes and advanced mathematics, there are still many puzzles about our universe that scientists have yet to solve. Uncovering the secrets of how our universe works, where it came from, and our place in the cosmos is an ongoing and exciting challenge.

Space

When people refer to space, they often mean outer space. Outer space begins about 60 miles (100 km) above Earth's surface. Although outer space seems empty, it contains bits of gas, dust, and other matter. Crowded regions, such as galaxies, contain many stars, planets, and black holes.

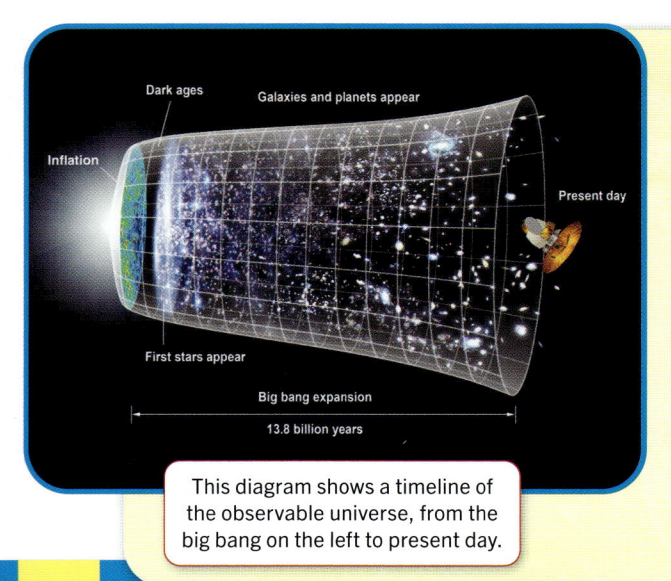

This diagram shows a timeline of the observable universe, from the big bang on the left to present day.

Time

Time is a measurement of periods between the past, present, and future. However, mathematicians and scientists now know that time is even more complicated. Einstein's theory of relativity says that time, space, and gravity are all connected. People experience time differently if they are closer or farther away from big sources of gravity or if they are moving at different speeds through space.

Spacetime

Space has three dimensions: length, width, and height. But according to Einstein, time is a fourth dimension connected to the others. To address this, scientists now talk about spacetime, a concept that combines space and time into one idea. Spacetime can be thought of as a fabric of the universe that gets bent and curved by objects with lots of mass. This curving of spacetime is also known as gravity.

Telescopes have helped scientists study the universe for more than 400 years.

The Solar System

Astronomers use their knowledge of physics to try to understand what's going on deep in space. The closest region of space to us is our solar system, which includes the planets, moons, asteroids, comets, and other objects held in orbit around our central star, the sun.

The solar system's four inner planets are small and made of solid rock.

Space Probes

Sending people into space is difficult, dangerous, and costly. So, scientists often send out uncrewed space probes or use powerful telescopes to study space. Space probes take close-up photos of planets or other space objects, scan them with radar and lasers to see what they are made of, and sometimes even land on them to investigate further.

Saturn

Earth

The *Cassini* probe was sent to study Saturn. The golden dome on top is a little lander called *Huygens*, which dropped onto Saturn's giant moon, Titan.

Mae Jemison
Born 1956

Mae Jemison is an engineer and medical doctor. In 1992, she became the first Black American woman to fly into space. She flew aboard the space shuttle *Endeavour* to study the effects of space flight on the body, including how it responds to weightlessness. Jemison was in space for eight days. After her time as an astronaut, she has worked to protect Earth's environment and make new technology safer.

HALL OF FAME

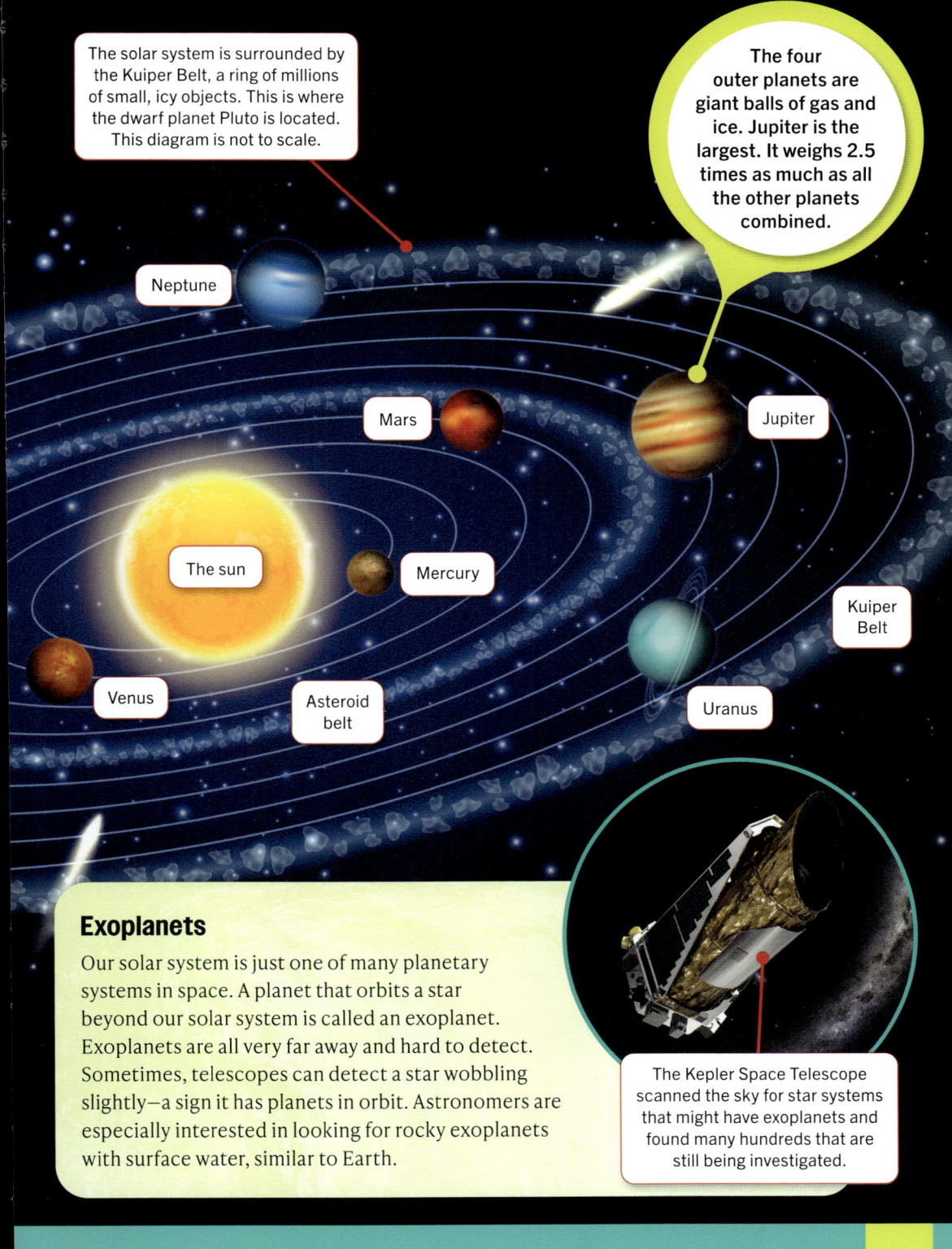

The solar system is surrounded by the Kuiper Belt, a ring of millions of small, icy objects. This is where the dwarf planet Pluto is located. This diagram is not to scale.

The four outer planets are giant balls of gas and ice. Jupiter is the largest. It weighs 2.5 times as much as all the other planets combined.

Neptune

Mars

Jupiter

The sun

Mercury

Kuiper Belt

Venus

Asteroid belt

Uranus

Exoplanets

Our solar system is just one of many planetary systems in space. A planet that orbits a star beyond our solar system is called an exoplanet. Exoplanets are all very far away and hard to detect. Sometimes, telescopes can detect a star wobbling slightly—a sign it has planets in orbit. Astronomers are especially interested in looking for rocky exoplanets with surface water, similar to Earth.

The Kepler Space Telescope scanned the sky for star systems that might have exoplanets and found many hundreds that are still being investigated.

DID YOU KNOW? Astronomers think that most stars have at least two planets orbiting them. That would mean there are far more planets in the universe than stars.

Gravity

What goes up must come down—because of the force of gravity. Gravity is the force of attraction between all objects that have mass. More massive bodies produce a stronger gravitational pull than less massive ones. The gravitational force between two objects also becomes stronger as the objects get closer together.

The force of Earth's gravity makes objects—including these skydivers—accelerate toward the middle of the planet.

Jupiter has several dozen moons that are all held in place by gravity.

Planetary Orbits

Gravity is the force that keeps a planet in orbit around a star and moons in orbit around a planet. The gravity of the larger body—a star, for example—pulls on the smaller one. A planet does not fall into its star because it also has momentum carrying it forward. This forward momentum combines with the downward pull of gravity to create a circular path.

Measuring Gravity

The strength of gravity acting between bodies depends on how much mass each has. The link between mass and the gravity it produces is a number called the gravitational constant (G). Since G is the same all over the universe, it can be used to calculate the pull of gravity between objects anywhere.

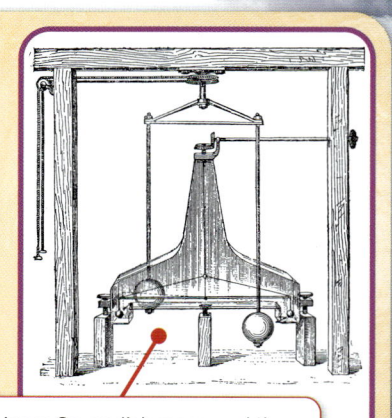

In the 1790s, Henry Cavendish measured the pull of gravity between large and small balls so he could calculate the density and mass of Earth.

Isaac Newton
1642–1727
The law of gravity was described by Newton in the mid-seventeenth century. According to some stories, he sat in his garden and saw an apple fall from a tree to the ground. At that moment, Newton understood how gravity acts between two bodies. Newton also explained the laws of motion, studied light, and created the reflecting telescope, improving on the refracting telescopes of his time.

The initial downward pull of gravity is soon balanced by the upward push of resistance from the air. The skydivers then stop accelerating but keep falling at a constant speed called terminal velocity.

Gravity is a two-way force, so as well as the skydivers falling to Earth, Earth is being pulled up toward the skydivers. However, the planet is so much bigger that it moves only a very tiny amount—the skydivers fall much farther!

DID YOU KNOW? The gravitational effect of a black hole is so powerful that even light cannot escape it—and that is why it is called a black hole.

Weight and Mass

Weight and mass are often used interchangeably, but they have different meanings. Mass is a measure of how much matter is in an object. That object's weight is the force of gravity pulling on it. Two objects of the same mass would weigh the same amount on Earth, but if one was on the moon it would weigh much less than the other. Still, the masses of both objects would still be the same.

Making Measurements

Weight is measured using scales that identify the force of gravity pulling down on an object. Mass is measured by how much an object will resist moving. When floating in space, an object will not push down on scales at all and so it is weightless, but since it has mass, it still needs a strong enough force to get it moving—and to stop it again.

The mass of these weights is a measure of the amount of matter in them. That never changes—even in space.

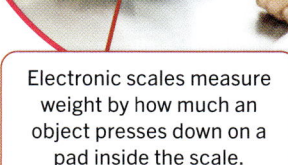

Electronic scales measure weight by how much an object presses down on a pad inside the scale.

Andrea Ghez
Born 1965

Andrea Ghez is an American astronomer who discovered the most massive thing in our galaxy. In 2012, Ghez showed that there is a black hole in the middle of the Milky Way called Sagittarius A*. Ghez used big telescopes to observe gravity from the black hole causing nearby stars to move very fast. She used those speeds to calculate the pull of the gravity from the black hole and found that Sagittarius A* had a mass four million times that of the sun!

HALL OF FAME

DID YOU KNOW? The pilots of fast fighter jets feel extra weight as they accelerate through a turn. The force that causes this extra weight is called a g-force.

Weightless in Space

Astronauts on the International Space Station (ISS) have no weight, since they are in constant free fall around the planet. But they still need to monitor their mass to make sure they stay healthy. This is measured using a special device that calculates how much force is needed to move their bodies against a spring with a known resistance.

An astronaut in space is weightless but not massless.

A weightlifter has to create a force stronger than gravity to lift the weight off the ground and above their head.

The weight of this bar depends on the force of gravity pulling it down to the ground. On Jupiter, where the gravity is stronger, its weight would be three times greater than on Earth!

Orbits and Weightlessness

An orbit is the path a less massive body follows around a more massive one. It is most familiar in astronomy—planets orbit stars and moons orbit planets. The gravity of the more massive, and usually larger, body holds the other body in its orbit. Artificial satellites and space stations orbit Earth using the same forces. Objects in orbit around much larger and more massive bodies—such as people orbiting Earth—appear to be weightless.

A Sense of Motion

Orbit can be described as a particular kind of falling. The gravity of a planet or star provides the centripetal force that pulls a body, such as a moon, planet, or satellite, toward it. On its own, this would make the body fall. But if the body is in motion, it will keep trying to move in a straight line, a property known as inertia. This inertia and the centripetal force combine to produce rotational movement. The object doesn't complete its fall but is instead in free fall. An orbiting satellite or spacecraft, including any astronauts inside, seems to float as if weightless.

Skydivers are in free fall while they descend toward Earth. A parachute provides a drag force that slows down their movement.

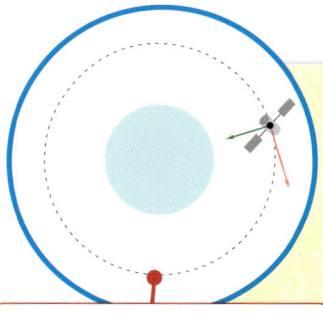

The orbital velocity is a balance between the pull of gravity and a satellite's inertia that would otherwise fling it out into space.

Orbital Velocity

The height of an orbit is called its altitude. The orbital velocity—the speed at which the object moves around the planet—depends on its altitude. A satellite orbiting near to Earth must move much faster than one that is in orbit farther away from Earth. If the satellite slows down, gravity will overcome inertia and pull the satellite down to Earth.

DID YOU KNOW? The ISS orbits 250 miles (400 km) above the surface of Earth.

It is not a lack of gravity that makes astronauts seem weightless. Gravity in Earth's orbit is only very slightly weaker than at Earth's surface.

Being weightless for a long time can slowly damage or weaken the human body.

Astronauts and spacecraft float in space, but they still have mass and momentum. They require the same forces to move around as they would on Earth.

Johannes Kepler
1571–1630

German astronomer Johannes Kepler discovered the relationship between motion and orbits by studying how planets move through the sky. Kepler discovered that planets do not have circular orbits. Rather, they move around the sun in elliptical, or slightly flattened circular, orbits. That means their distance from the sun constantly changes. Planets move more quickly when they're closer to the sun and more slowly when they're farther away.

HALL OF FAME

13

What Is Matter?

Matter is anything in the universe that takes up space and has mass. All matter is made of tiny particles called atoms. Your body, your home, trees, oceans, rocks, and everything else on planet Earth are made of matter. In space, matter often gathers into planets, moons, and stars. Matter always contains some amount of energy. Adding or removing energy can cause matter to change its form, or state.

The most familiar matter that changes between solid, liquid, and gas is water. On Earth, it is solid as ice, liquid as water, and gas as steam.

States of Matter

Matter exists in three main states—solid, liquid, and gas. These states are the result of how atoms move within the matter. Matter changes state as it becomes hotter or colder. In a cold solid, the atoms are arranged into a fixed shape and volume. Solids melt into liquids as they warm up. Liquids have a fixed volume but no fixed shape. Heating a liquid until it boils makes a gas, which has neither a fixed shape nor a fixed volume.

Matter and Energy

When matter is heated, heat energy makes the atoms vibrate. As matter cools, its atoms move less. Matter can also lose or gain energy in a chemical change. A chemical change rearranges the atoms into different substances. For example, burning a log changes it from wood into smoke, gas, and ash.

An explosion is a rapid chemical change that transforms the physical nature of matter. Some matter is converted to smoke or gases. A lot of energy is released as heat.

DID YOU KNOW? There is a fourth state of matter called plasma. It can be created when a gas gets very hot or is affected by electricity. The sun is made of plasma.

John Dalton
1766–1844

The original idea of matter being made of atoms dates back to ancient Greece. In 1801, British scientist John Dalton introduced modern atomic theory. He suggested that in chemical reactions, atoms of different types combine to make different substances. He noted that they always combine in the same proportions to make the new substance.

Matter can be pushed and pulled by forces. These forces can make matter move and change shape.

Although we cannot see it, we are surrounded by matter all the time in the form of gases in the air.

The atoms that make up matter are made of smaller particles called protons, neutrons, and electrons.

15

Dark Matter

Astronomers have measured all of the matter in the universe that we can see, including all of the stars and galaxies. But they have found that the mass of the universe is much greater than the total mass of all of the stars and galaxies. Scientists have named this missing material dark matter.

Mystery Matter and Energy

Scientists believe that there is about five times more dark matter than ordinary matter. But there is also something even more mysterious called dark energy. Dark energy was discovered in 1998. It makes up around two-thirds of the matter and energy in the universe. It is causing space to expand, but physicists do not really understand it yet.

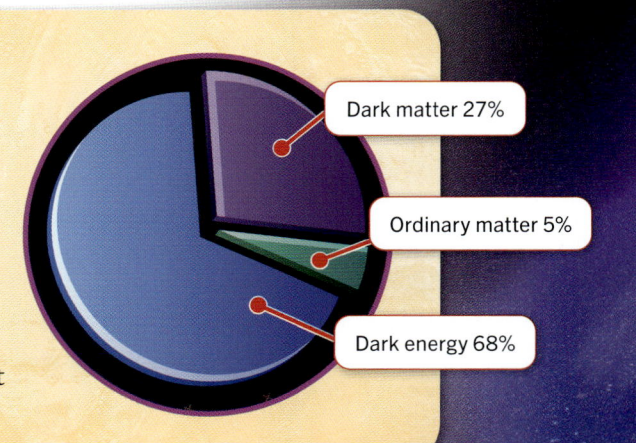

Dark matter 27%

Ordinary matter 5%

Dark energy 68%

Detectors

Dark matter is called dark because it does not produce light or any kind of radiation. Nor is it affected by electromagnetism in any way. The only force that seems to affect dark matter is gravity. The search for dark matter is very difficult. No one has found any yet. Some dark matter detectors are looking for tiny particles that may exist all around us now but do not show up in standard tests.

Dark matter detectors are deep underground to shield them from all other particles and radiation.

DID YOU KNOW? One explanation of dark matter is that it is the effect of gravity from other universes influencing our own.

Astronomers looking at how galaxies spin around realized that galaxies move faster than they should. That means they have more mass than we can see. This extra mass is dark matter.

Astronomers think that some dark matter might be undetectable objects in the halo around the edge of a galaxy.

If a galaxy were made only from the kind of ordinary matter that we can detect, all of its stars would be flung out into deep space as it spun around. There wouldn't be enough mass or gravity to hold the galaxy together.

Vera Rubin
1928–2016

In 1979, after studying the stars in Andromeda, the nearest big galaxy to our own, Vera Rubin showed that dark matter makes up a lot of the mass of galaxies. She calculated the speed at which stars were moving as they orbited the center of the galaxy. She found that stars at the edge were moving much too fast for the known mass of the galaxy. Rubin calculated that galaxies must have between 5 and 10 times more mass than we can see.

HALL OF FAME

Antimatter

Almost everything in our universe is made from particles of matter. A very small number of particles in our universe are made of antimatter, matter's mirror image. Each particle of matter has an opposite antimatter version. But antimatter is often very hard to make. When matter and antimatter touch, they destroy each other.

Antimatter and the Big Bang

Both matter and antimatter were created during the big bang. But when both collide, they destroy each other. Some scientists speculate that there could have been slightly more matter than antimatter particles. That could have been enough to create a universe made mostly of matter.

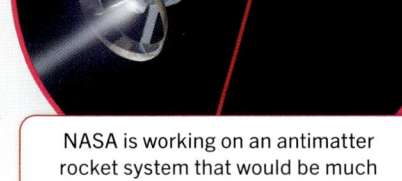

NASA is working on an antimatter rocket system that would be much more efficient than current rockets.

Using Antimatter to Detect Disease

Positrons are the antimatter equivalent of electrons. Positron-emission tomography (PET) scans are a tool doctors use to detect cancer. A particle accelerator is used to cause a type of sugar molecule to become radioactive and release positrons. When injected into the body, the molecule travels and finds cancer cells, which then show up on scans.

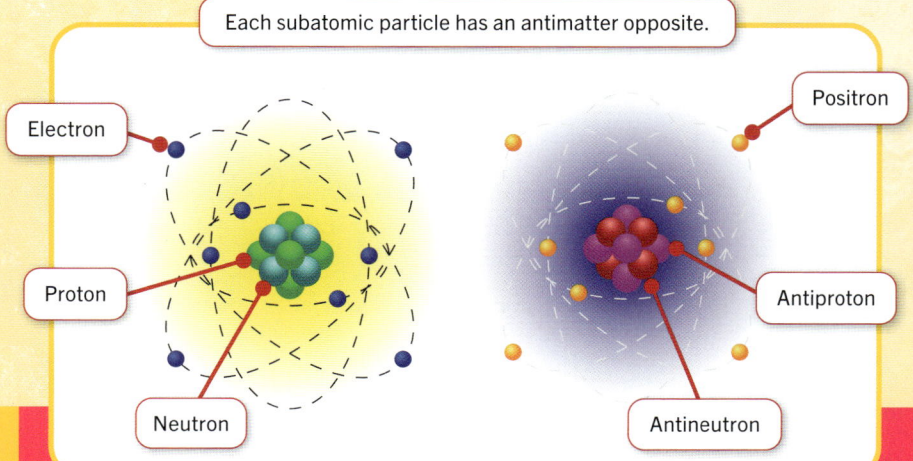

Each subatomic particle has an antimatter opposite.

Electron

Positron

Proton

Antiproton

Neutron

Antineutron

Paul Dirac
1902–1984

Paul Dirac was the first physicist to predict antimatter. In 1928, he made the discovery accidentally while writing an equation to describe an electron moving at almost the speed of light. Two possible solutions to his equation included both a negatively charged electron and its positively charged opposite, a positron. Dirac won the Nobel Prize in 1933.

Powerful thunderstorms over Earth create electric fields, which in turn produce gamma ray flashes.

NASA's Fermi Gamma-Ray Space Telescope monitors gamma rays in outer space. It also observes gamma ray flashes from thunderstorms over Earth.

Gamma ray flashes create antimatter. This burst of antimatter was captured by a NASA spacecraft in 2012.

DID YOU KNOW? Ordinary bananas produce antimatter. They are rich in potassium, which decays and produces a positron about once every 75 minutes.

Electromagnetism

Electromagnetism is one of the basic forces in the universe. It produces electricity, magnetism, and light. It also helps hold matter together. All particles have an electric charge. They can be positive, negative, or neutral. Objects with opposite charges are attracted to each other, while those with like charges push each other away. The charge comes from subatomic particles, most often the negatively charged electron. Anything that gains extra electrons has a negative charge, while anything that loses them has a positive charge.

Light Radiation

Visible light, infrared light, radio waves, and X-rays are all forms of electromagnetic radiation. When electrons in an atom give out energy, they release a burst of light or another form of radiation. When that radiation hits another atom, it might be absorbed by an electron or reflected off again.

A laser is an instrument that can produce a powerful beam of light. The word *laser* stands for light amplification by stimulated emission of radiation.

Batteries use chemical reactions to produce electric currents.

Electric Currents

Electricity is a flow of charged particles—most often electrons. The electrons move from an area where there are many electrons to a place where there are fewer. Batteries and other sources of electricity keep the current flowing by continually adding more electrons at one end and removing them from the other.

DID YOU KNOW? While the force of electromagnetism is many trillions of times stronger than gravity, it is more than 100 times weaker than the strong nuclear force.

The body's motion is powered by electromagnetic forces in muscles. Charged particles called ions move through the muscle cells, making them change shape and contract the muscle.

The electromagnetic force helps keep atoms separated from one another. It pushes an atom's outermost electrons away from those of nearby atoms. This is why a baseball bounces off a bat instead of going through it.

Electromagnetic force holds atoms together, keeping the negatively charged electrons bound to the positively charged nucleus.

Hans Christian Ørsted
1777–1851

This Danish scientist discovered the link between electricity and magnetism, and thus he created a new area of physics called electromagnetism. Ørsted discovered that the magnetic needle of a compass will swing toward a wire carrying an electric current but then swing back to point north when the current is turned off. In 1820, he published his finding that an electric current produces a magnetic field around the wire through which it travels.

HALL OF FAME

21

Telescopes

The word *telescope* means far seeing in ancient Greek. A telescope is used to magnify objects that are too far away to see clearly or at all with the naked eye. It does this by collecting light or other electromagnetic waves from the object and focusing these waves into a clear, bright image. It then magnifies that image to show the details.

Refracting and Reflecting Telescopes

A refracting telescope works by refracting, or bending, light. A large lens at the front, called the objective lens, collects light entering the telescope and focuses it at the far end of the tube onto another lens. This small lens, called the eyepiece, magnifies the image. A reflecting telescope uses curved mirrors in place of lenses to redirect the light. Most modern telescopes used for astronomy are reflecting telescopes.

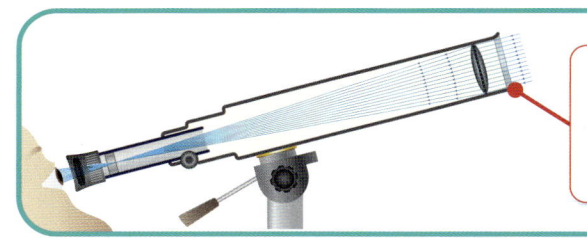

The light rays in a simple refracting telescope cross over at the focal point of the first lens, so the image produced is upside down. Another lens flips the image right-side up again.

Radio Telescopes

Reflecting and refracting telescopes are both optical telescopes—they work with light. Other telescopes work with different types of electromagnetic radiation. Dish-like radio telescopes pick up radio waves coming from objects in space. The waves are reflected by the curved dish onto a feed in the middle.

As well as studying stars, galaxies, and black holes, radio telescopes scan for radio waves that could be produced by intelligent beings elsewhere in space.

DID YOU KNOW? The James Webb Space Telescope uses infrared energy waves from deep space to see more than 13.8 billion light-years away.

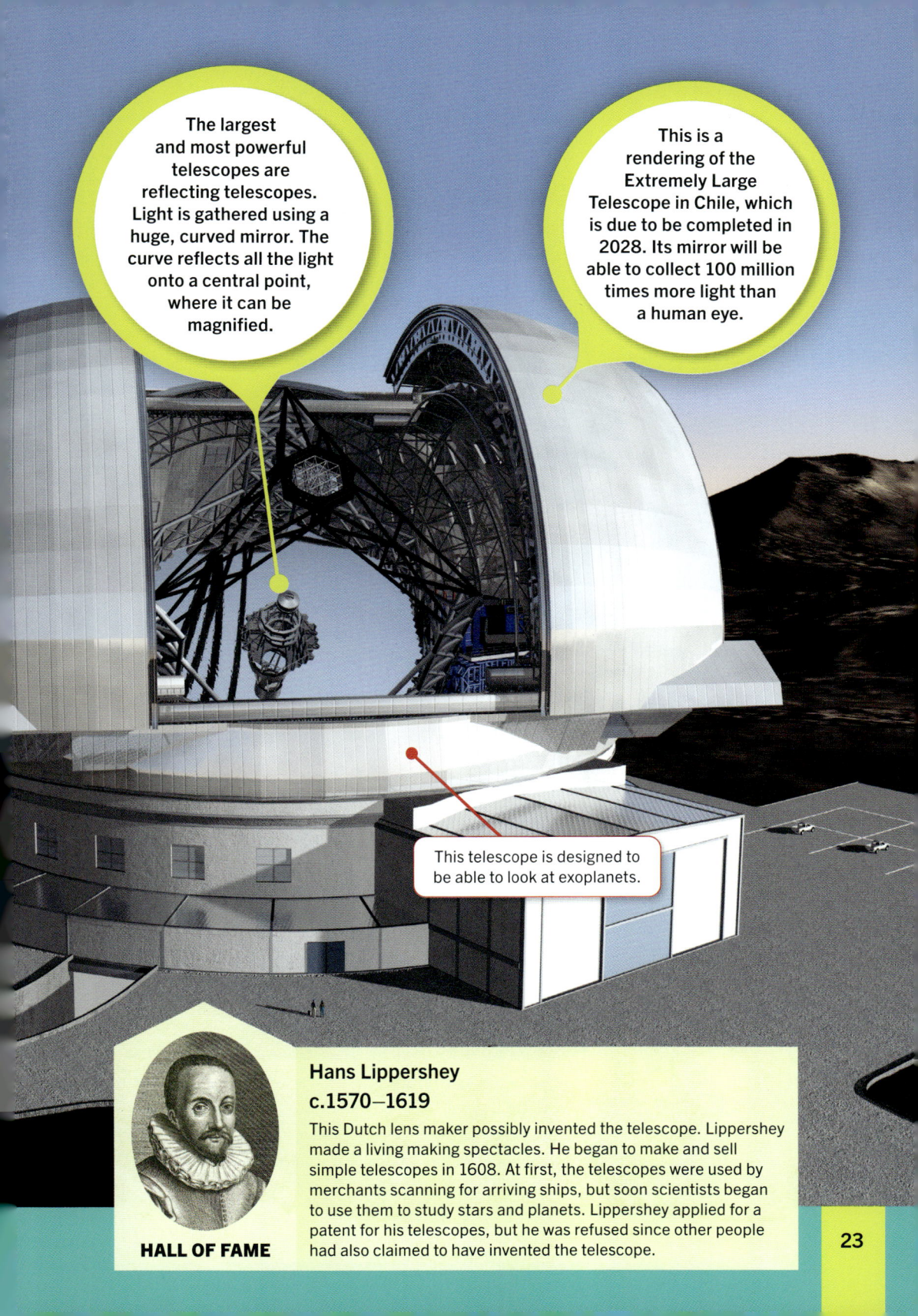

The largest and most powerful telescopes are reflecting telescopes. Light is gathered using a huge, curved mirror. The curve reflects all the light onto a central point, where it can be magnified.

This is a rendering of the Extremely Large Telescope in Chile, which is due to be completed in 2028. Its mirror will be able to collect 100 million times more light than a human eye.

This telescope is designed to be able to look at exoplanets.

Hans Lippershey
c.1570–1619

This Dutch lens maker possibly invented the telescope. Lippershey made a living making spectacles. He began to make and sell simple telescopes in 1608. At first, the telescopes were used by merchants scanning for arriving ships, but soon scientists began to use them to study stars and planets. Lippershey applied for a patent for his telescopes, but he was refused since other people had also claimed to have invented the telescope.

HALL OF FAME

23

The Big Bang

The big bang theory is the leading explanation of how the universe began 13.8 billion years ago. The big bang event caused the sudden and rapid expansion of the universe from an extremely hot and dense state called a singularity. As the universe expanded, it cooled enough to begin forming the particles, atoms, and molecules that make up every object we can see in space.

The expansion of the universe following the big bang dates back nearly 13.8 billion years.

The Cosmic Microwave Background

Cosmic microwave background (CMB) radiation is the heat and light that was left over following the big bang. It has traveled billions of light-years through the expanding universe to reach Earth. We can see this radiation using special telescopes. Mapping the CMB helps scientists learn how the early universe formed.

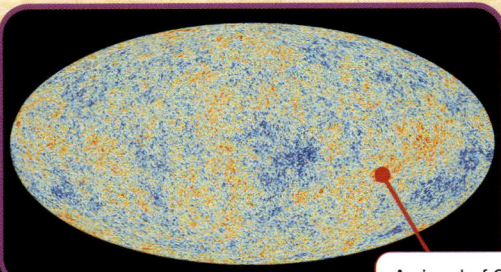

A visual of CMB radiation captured by ESA's Planck space telescope

Georges Lemaître
1894–1966

Georges Lemaître was a Belgian cosmologist. In 1927, he wrote a paper that suggested the universe was expanding. Years later, astronomer Edwin Hubble proved that Lemaître was correct by observing the light from distant stars. In 1931, Lemaître proposed the first big bang creation theory by reversing that expansion through time.

HALL OF FAME

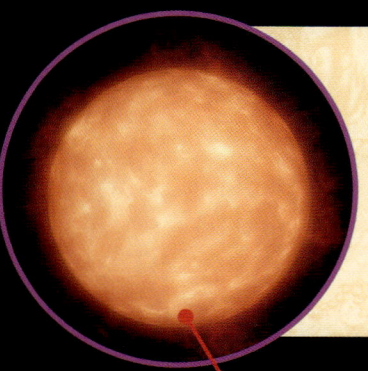

Pressing Rewind on the Big Bang

Scientists who study the origins of the universe are called cosmologists. Some cosmologists use computer programs to create virtual universes. One supercomputer was programmed to create 4,000 different versions of the initial expansion of the universe. Scientists hope to successfully reconstruct the universe immediately after the big bang.

Scientists believe that the first stars to form in the universe were somewhere between 10 and 300 times bigger than the sun.

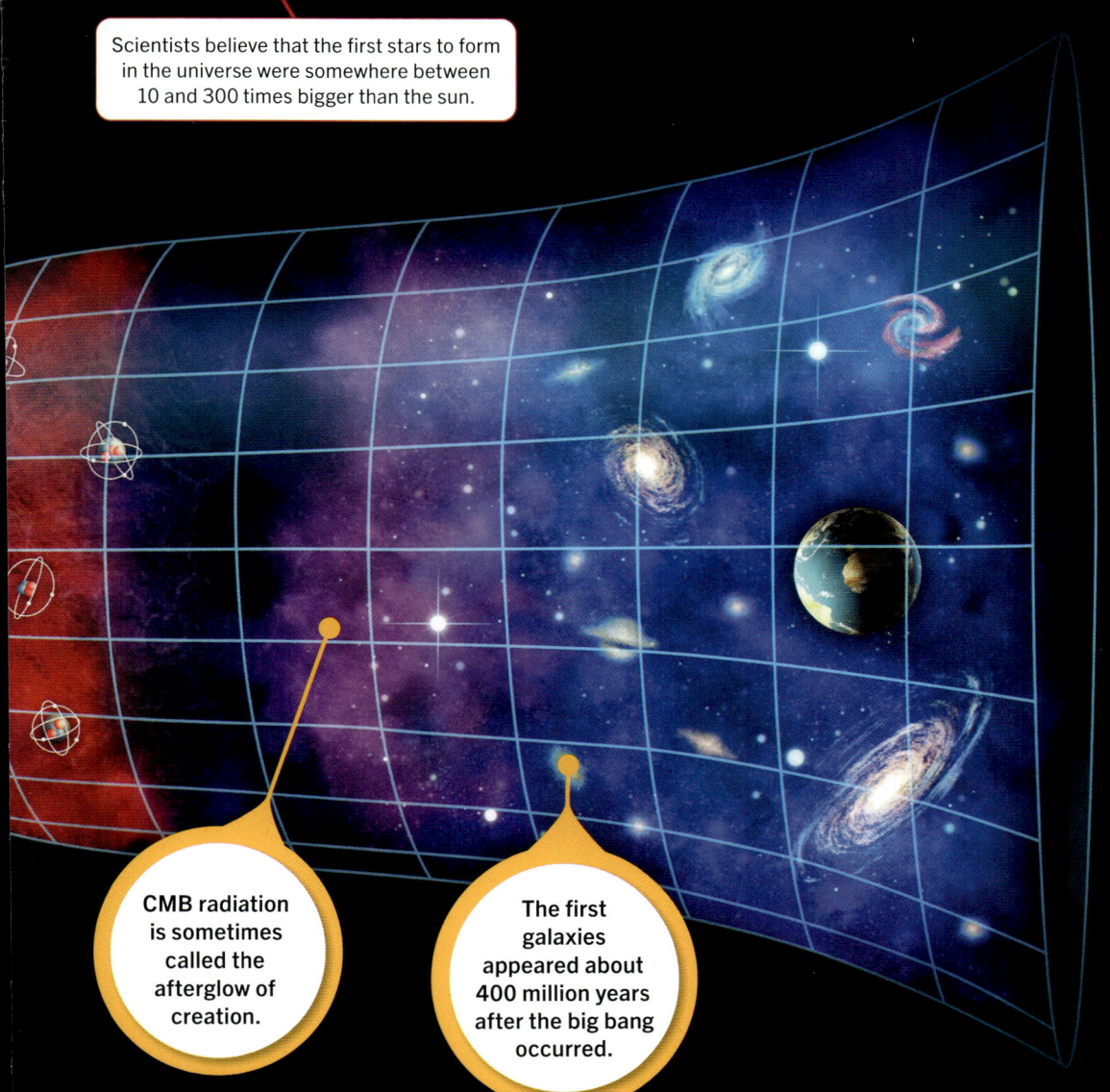

CMB radiation is sometimes called the afterglow of creation.

The first galaxies appeared about 400 million years after the big bang occurred.

DID YOU KNOW? Even though the first atoms were created only minutes after the big bang, scientists believe the first stars didn't appear until nearly 200 million years later.

Stars

The sun is our nearest star. It is the source of all the light and heat that keeps Earth warm and habitable. Despite being very special to us, this star is no different than many, many trillions of others. It is a ball of hydrogen plasma, or superhot and electrified gas.

Fusion Power

The heat and light of a star comes from nuclear fusion reactions happening deep inside the core, or central zone. The temperature and pressure there are so high that atoms are squashed together so their nuclei fuse. Through several steps, four atoms of hydrogen form one of helium, giving out a lot of energy as they do so.

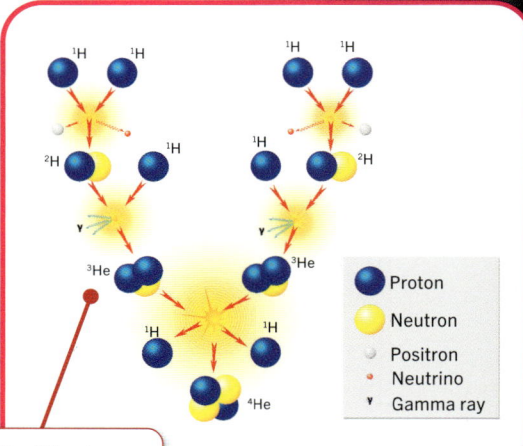

Every second, the sun converts more than 672 million tons (610 million t) of hydrogen into helium through nuclear fusion.

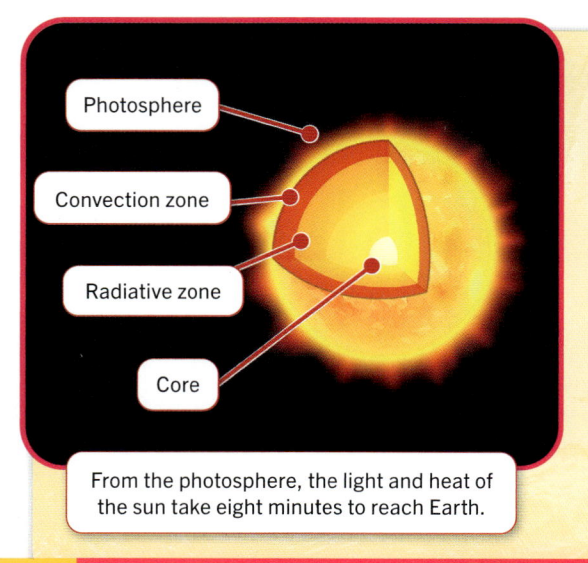

Photosphere

Convection zone

Radiative zone

Core

From the photosphere, the light and heat of the sun take eight minutes to reach Earth.

Inside a Star

A star has different layers. The core is where fusion happens. The energy from there leaks out into the next layer, called the radiative zone. The plasma is so tightly packed that from there it takes thousands to millions of years for the heat and light to get to the convection zone. Here, the plasma is churning like a pan of boiling water, and the heat rises to the surface, or photosphere, where it pours out into space.

A star is surrounded by a layer of gases called a corona.

Sometimes, an enormous fountain of plasma bursts from the surface of a star. The plasma is pulled back in by the star's magnetism, forming a bright loop bigger than Earth.

Darker patches on the sun are called sunspots. The temperature of these magnetically active areas is only 7,000 degrees Fahrenheit (3,900°C). The rest of the surface is about 10,000°F (5,500°C)!

Cecilia Payne-Gaposchkin
1900–1979

British astronomer Cecilia Payne-Gaposchkin figured out in 1925 that the sun and most other stars are made from hydrogen and helium. This was the first big step in understanding how stars generate light and heat. At first, astronomers were unwilling to accept her findings, but she was soon proved right.

HALL OF FAME

27

The Planets

The eight planets of our solar system are held in orbit around the sun by the sun's gravity. They are at different distances from the sun, so their orbits take different amounts of time. Neptune is farthest from the sun and takes 165 Earth years to make a single orbit. Earth's orbit is about 365 days, or 1 Earth year. Mercury's orbit takes only 88 Earth days.

Giant Planets

The four outer planets are much larger than the inner four. Jupiter and Saturn are gas giants formed mostly from hydrogen and helium around a small core of rock and ice. Uranus and Neptune have thin outer shells of hydrogen and helium surrounding dense icy water and ammonia. They each have a larger, icy, rocky core. They are known as ice giant planets.

Saturn is famous for its rings. These are made of rocky dust and chunks of ice. Although the rings are hundreds of thousands of miles across, they are only about 300 feet (100 m) thick.

Rocky Planets

The four inner planets are rocky worlds. Earth is the third from the sun and the largest, closely followed by Venus. Mars is about half this size, while Mercury, the smallest planet, is a third of Earth's size. Mercury and Venus are scorchingly hot, while Mars is a cold and dry place. Earth is the only planet where there is always liquid water on the surface.

Mars looks red even when seen with the naked eye. The red comes from the iron-rich sand and rocks that cover the planet.

DID YOU KNOW? At least nine rocky bodies in our solar system do not quite qualify as planets. These are called dwarf planets. The largest is Pluto.

As the planets grew, their gravity swept up the gas, dust, and ice around them, leaving the empty space we see today.

The planets formed through collisions of small lumps of rock that stuck together due to the pull of gravity. Gradually, the planets grew bigger and bigger, becoming round.

The planets formed 4.6 billion years ago from a vast disk of dust, ice, and gas whirling around the young sun. The heavier rocky dust moved closer to the star. The lighter gases and ice drifted farther away.

Moogega Cooper
Born 1985

American planetary scientist Moogega Cooper is part of the team that controls the *Perseverance* rover that landed on Mars in 2020. The wheeled, car-sized robot examines rocks in search of chemicals that are made by living things. Cooper made sure that *Perseverance* did not carry germs from Earth that might contaminate Mars and either affect any possible Martian life or mislead future scientists.

HALL OF FAME

The Moon

Earth's nearest neighbor in space is the moon. It is a natural satellite of Earth that is about a quarter of our planet's size. While other planets have moons, and a few are bigger than ours, Earth's moon is the largest satellite in comparison with its host planet. The moon is about 239,000 miles (385,000 km) away—a distance about 30 times the width of Earth.

Apollo Landings

The moon is the only space body that humans have visited. The Apollo missions each took three days to reach the moon. Only 12 people have ever walked on the moon's surface. No one has been back for more than 50 years, but there are several plans to return to the moon and even set up a permanent base there.

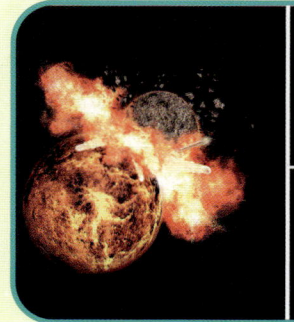

An important job of Apollo astronauts was to collect moon rocks for experts to study back on Earth.

Making the Moon

Most astronomers think the moon formed around 4.5 billion years ago when a planet about the size of Mars smashed into Earth. The planet, named Theia, and a large part of Earth vaporized on impact, forming a cloud of rock and gas around Earth. This cooled and clumped together to form the moon. Moon rock is similar to, but not exactly the same as, Earth rock because it is mixed with the smashed-up rock of Theia.

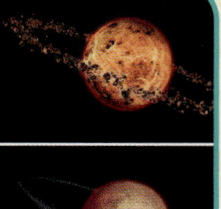

DID YOU KNOW? The moon's gravity creates the tides in Earth's oceans. It pulls on the ocean water, creating a bulge that moves as Earth turns.

Gerard Kuiper
1905–1973

Dutch astronomer Gerard Kuiper made many discoveries about the solar system. He spent most of his life working in the United States, where he became an expert in observing planets and moons. He discovered two moons around Uranus and Neptune, and his expertise helped determine the best place to land on the moon for the Apollo missions. The Kuiper Belt, made of millions of icy objects beyond Neptune, is named for him.

The dark areas of the moon are called lunar seas. People once thought they were areas of water, but we know today that they are low-lying regions covered in dark rock that erupted from lunar volcanoes long ago.

The moon turns on its axis once for each orbit of Earth, so we always see the same side.

The moon has very little atmosphere. Its gravity is only one-sixth as strong as Earth's, and so any gases it once had have long since drifted away into space.

Comets and Asteroids

In addition to planets, the solar system has many millions of smaller objects. The inner solar system has asteroids made of a mixture of rock, metals, and some ice. Comets come from the cold outer solar system and are made of ice mixed with rock dust. The many craters we see on the moon are evidence of asteroids and comets crashing into it long ago. Similar space objects have also hit Earth in its past.

Asteroids

Most asteroids orbit in the asteroid belt, a vast ring of rocks that circles the sun between the orbits of Mars and Jupiter. The largest object in the asteroid belt is the dwarf planet Ceres, which is about 580 miles (930 km) across.

Asteroids contain the same materials that made the rocky planets billions of years ago.

This crater in the Arizona desert was made by a meteor.

Meteors and Meteorites

Any space rock that enters Earth's atmosphere is called a meteor. Most meteors are specks of dust. Friction created by moving through the air as they fall makes them very hot. Most burn up, appearing to us as shooting stars. Occasionally, larger rocks reach the ground before burning up completely, and these are called meteorites. Impacts from a large meteorite are very rare but can be catastrophic. The dinosaurs died out after an asteroid 6 miles (10 km) wide hit the planet 66 million years ago.

Caroline Herschel
1750–1848

Caroline Herschel became an astronomer with her older brother, William. Working together and separately, they identified Uranus, discovered many asteroids, and created very accurate star maps. Herschel's search for comets and nebulae, or huge gas clouds, led her to discover at least five comets.

A comet's tail is millions of miles long. It always faces away from the sun, so the tail is in front of the comet as it flies back into deep space.

Comets develop a tail as they approach the sun. Ice in the comet melts, freeing particles of dust. The sun illuminates the dust, making a bright streak in the sky.

The lumpy nucleus of a comet looks like a dirty snowball. Comets form in the colder parts of the solar system and can be knocked toward the sun by collisions. Many comets take hundreds of years to make one orbit around the sun.

DID YOU KNOW? The two moons of Mars, Phobos and Deimos, are thought to be asteroids that were captured by the Red Planet's gravity.

33

Galaxies

Stars are not evenly spread through the universe. Instead, they cluster in huge groups called galaxies. The space between galaxies is mostly empty. Our galaxy, called the Milky Way, is 100,000 light-years wide. That means it takes 100,000 years for the light from a star on one side of the galaxy to reach the opposite side.

Our solar system is located toward the edge of one of our galaxy's spiral arms. When we look toward the middle of the galaxy, we can see a pale streak running across the sky that is made up of the light of billions of stars.

Spirals and Disks

The Milky Way has at least 100 billion stars. These stars are arranged in a spiral, spinning around a central point. Many galaxies have this spiral shape. Old galaxies that formed a long time ago are normally oval or egg-shaped. The largest galaxies, with perhaps 100 times as many stars as ours, have a cloudlike irregular shape. They are thought to have been made by several smaller galaxies colliding and combining.

Jacobus Kapteyn
1851–1922
Dutch astronomer Jacobus Kapteyn discovered that the Milky Way is rotating. He noticed that stars in one direction in the sky seemed to be moving faster than those in the other. He realized that he was seeing some stars on the edge of a great rotating disk and others nearer the middle.

HALL OF FAME

The name Milky Way has origins in ancient Greece. Today's English word *galaxy* comes from the Greek word for milk.

Rogue Planets

Not all planets orbit a star. Some planets fly through space outside the gravity of any stellar system. These are called rogue planets. Scientists are not sure how rogue planets were formed. Perhaps they were pushed out of orbit, or they might have formed in a gas cloud that did not also create a star. However they came to be, some scientists think there are even more rogue planets in our galaxy than planets orbiting stars.

The Milky Way has different names around the world. In China, it is known as the Silver River, and the Vikings called it the World Tree.

Scientists believe there is a supermassive black hole at the center of each galaxy.

DID YOU KNOW? No one is quite sure how many galaxies the known universe has. It could be as few as 200 billion or as many as 2 trillion!

Space and Time

Strange things happen at the speed of light. As objects approach the speed of light, they become more massive and time passes more slowly. The laws of physics described by Newton and other classical physicists don't seem to work anymore. It took one of the world's greatest physicists, Albert Einstein, to explain this with his famous theory of general relativity. Einstein's theory joins space, time, and energy together to show why the speed of light is always the same in the vacuum of space and how gravity really works.

Speed of Light

The traditional laws of motion say that a light beam shining out of a rocket should be moving at the speed of light, plus the speed of the rocket. But when physicists measure light, it always moves at the same speed, regardless of where it comes from! It is a law of physics that light always moves at the same speed in a vacuum— nearly 186,000 miles per second (300,000 kps).

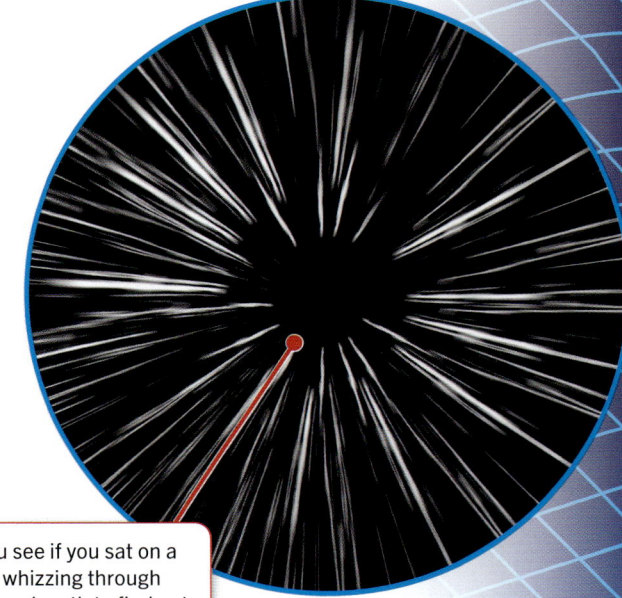

What would you see if you sat on a beam of light whizzing through space? Einstein used math to find out.

Albert Einstein
1879–1955

Though Albert Einstein is now considered one of the greatest physicists of all time, he was not always a good student. Einstein was bored at school, and his teachers did not think he was very smart. After school, he had a quiet office job and used his spare time to work on physics. Only after publishing his early theories in 1905 did Einstein get a job as a full-time scientist.

HALL OF FAME

Time Changes

Imagine twin brothers. One twin flies in a spacecraft for a journey at nearly the speed of light. When he returns home, he would be surprised to find that his twin brother would be much older than him. This strange problem is described by Einstein's theory of relativity. When an object moves through space very quickly, its movement through time slows down. On Earth, things move too slowly for us to be able to perceive any changes in time. However, the changes can be measured out in space, where stars and galaxies are moving very quickly.

Einstein's theory also says that mass bends, or warps, spacetime. This bending is what creates gravity.

Anything moving past this star will swing toward it. This is because it is moving through curved spacetime.

Imagine an asteroid traveling in a straight line though flat space. When flat space is warped into a curve by the sun, all the straight lines running through it also become curved. The asteroid's straight path swings toward the sun when it reaches the warped space.

DID YOU KNOW? People on the ISS age slightly more slowly than people on Earth because the astronauts are moving through space so quickly.

Black Holes

Some stars collapse when they reach the end of their life cycle, and all their matter gets crushed into a very small space by gravity. This creates a black hole. The matter in a black hole is so dense and its gravity so strong that it pulls anything that gets too close inside it. Not even light is fast enough to escape a black hole's gravity. Objects that are too far from the black hole to be sucked inside may still get pulled into orbit.

Black Hole Sizes

Black holes come in many sizes. Stellar mass black holes are born from the death of stars more than 20 times larger than our sun. Supermassive black holes live at the center of nearly every galaxy. They have at least 100,000 times more mass than the sun. Intermediate mass black holes are somewhere in between, but these are also very rare.

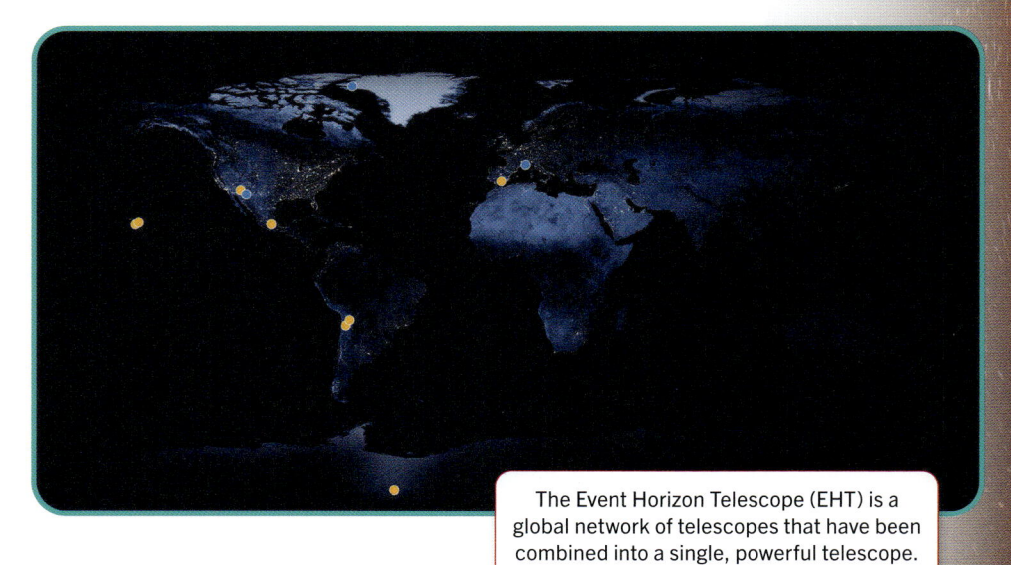

The Event Horizon Telescope (EHT) is a global network of telescopes that have been combined into a single, powerful telescope.

Karl Schwarzschild
1873–1916

Karl Schwarzschild was a German astronomer. He wrote two papers about Albert Einstein's theory of relativity, and in 1915, he provided the correct solution to Einstein's gravitational field equations. His work laid the foundation for the later study of black holes. Interestingly, Schwarzschild himself did not believe black holes actually existed.

HALL OF FAME

Some black holes are surrounded by an accretion disk made of matter and gas that orbits the black hole.

The center of a black hole is a point where matter becomes infinitely dense. This is called a singularity.

The event horizon is a black hole's surface. Anything that passes beyond the event horizon must move into the black hole, including light.

Sagittarius A*

Sagittarius A* is the supermassive black hole at the center of our galaxy, the Milky Way. Everything in the galaxy swirls around it, including our solar system.

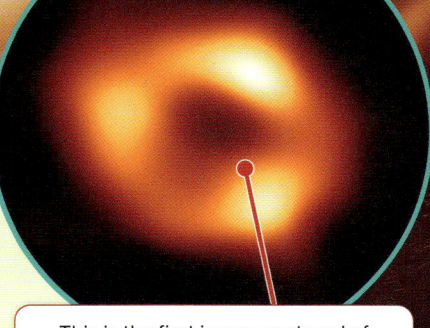

This is the first image captured of Sagittarius A*, the supermassive black hole at the center of the Milky Way.

DID YOU KNOW? Some black holes may have formed even before the first stars appeared. Scientists call these primordial black holes, but none have been found yet.

The End of the Universe

Cosmologists believe that the universe began 13.8 billion years ago in the big bang and that it has been expanding ever since. Scientists agree that at some point, the universe will come to an end. But they disagree about how and when that will happen.

Big Crunch, Big Rip, or Big Freeze

Some scientists believe gravity could eventually overcome the universe's expansion and cause it to collapse in on itself in a big crunch. Other scientists think the universe may expand far enough to tear apart in a big rip. As the universe expands, it loses energy. Some scientists believe that once all that energy is spread out evenly, the universe may end in an extreme frozen state called a big freeze.

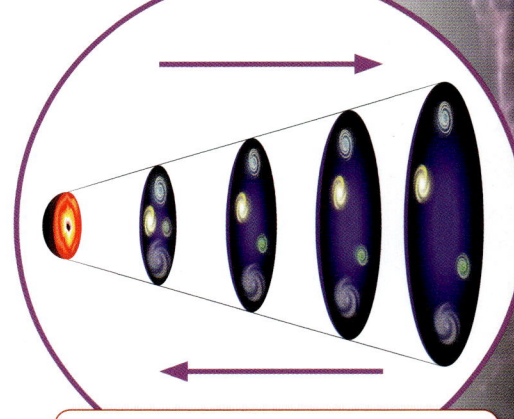

A visual imagining of the big crunch showing expansion and contraction over time

The Big Bounce

A variation of the big crunch end-of-the-universe theory is the big bounce. Just before the universe collapses in on itself, it may be saved by a quantum process that reverses the crunch. Another big bang would then begin, and a brand-new universe would be born.

The Hubble Space Telescope shows that the universe is expanding much faster than scientists expected.

DID YOU KNOW? Scientists don't think the universe will end for many billions or even trillions of years.

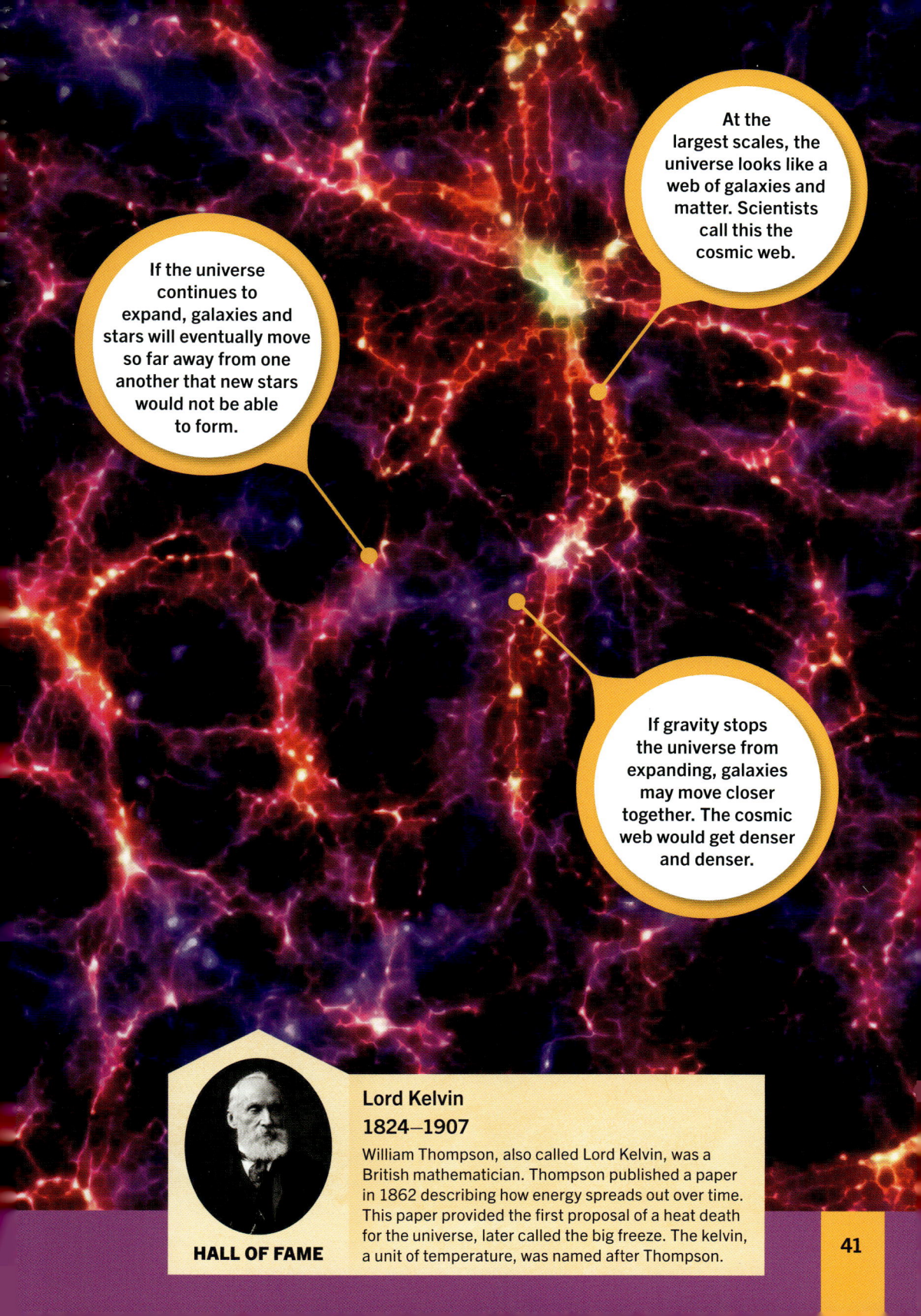

At the largest scales, the universe looks like a web of galaxies and matter. Scientists call this the cosmic web.

If the universe continues to expand, galaxies and stars will eventually move so far away from one another that new stars would not be able to form.

If gravity stops the universe from expanding, galaxies may move closer together. The cosmic web would get denser and denser.

Lord Kelvin
1824–1907

William Thompson, also called Lord Kelvin, was a British mathematician. Thompson published a paper in 1862 describing how energy spreads out over time. This paper provided the first proposal of a heat death for the universe, later called the big freeze. The kelvin, a unit of temperature, was named after Thompson.

HALL OF FAME

41

An Expanding Universe

Just like the universe itself, our understanding of it is constantly expanding. New tools, such as the James Webb Space Telescope, are helping scientists learn more about the past, present, and future of space. But there is still much to learn. Unraveling these mysteries will continue to inspire generations of people from now until the end of time.

The Future of Space Exploration

NASA has been at the forefront of space exploration for more than 60 years. This U.S. space agency has helped uncover mysteries as well as posed new questions about Earth's future. NASA has future plans to send astronauts to the moon's south pole and spacecraft to Jupiter's moon, Europa, to search for signs of life.

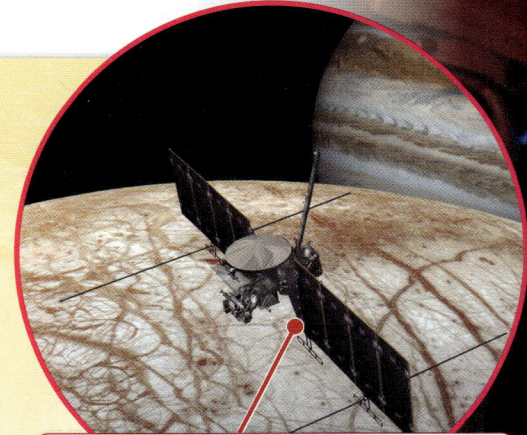

NASA's *Europa Clipper* spacecraft was launched in 2024. It will arrive at Europa in 2030.

The James Webb Space Telescope can see infrared light from just after the big bang.

The James Webb Space Telescope

The James Webb Space Telescope is a project led by NASA that hopes to uncover some of the biggest mysteries of the universe. The telescope is the largest ever built. It is studying every phase of the history of the universe from the big bang to the formation of our solar system.

The Parker Solar Probe

The Parker Solar Probe is an uncrewed spacecraft that entered the sun's corona in 2021. The probe's mission is to complete closer and closer orbits of the sun and record observations. Over 7 years, the probe will complete 24 orbits around the sun.

Review and Reflect

Now that you've read about space and time, let's review what you've learned. Use the following questions to reflect on your newfound knowledge and integrate it with what you already knew.

Check for Understanding

1. How do scientists learn about outer space? *(See pp. 6–7)*

2. What can cause gravity to become stronger? *(See pg. 8)*

3. What's the difference between mass and weight? *(See pg. 10)*

4. Why does an object in orbit appear to be weightless? *(See pp. 12–13)*

5. What are the four states of matter? What can cause matter to change state? *(See pg. 14)*

6. What clues make scientists think that dark matter exists? *(See pp. 16–17)*

7. Name and describe at least two kinds of telescopes. *(See pg. 22)*

8. What do cosmologists study? *(See pg. 25)*

9. Name and describe the layers of a star. *(See pg. 26)*

10. What is the difference between rocky planets and gas giants? *(See pp. 28–29)*

11. How do astronomers think the moon was formed? *(See pg. 30)*

12. Explain the differences between comets, asteroids, and meteors. *(See pg. 32)*

13. List two characteristics of the Milky Way. *(See pg. 34)*

14. Describe a black hole. How do black holes form? *(See pp. 38–39)*

15. Name and describe one theory about how the universe could end. *(See pg. 40)*

Making Connections

1. Name and describe one tool or concept scientists needed to learn more about our universe. Why was that tool necessary?

2. Choose two people mentioned in the Hall of Fame sidebars. What does their work have in common? What is a difference between them?

3. In what ways are solar systems and galaxies alike and different?

4. What is the difference between exoplanets and rogue planets? How are they similar?

5. How are antimatter, dark matter, and matter different? Why do we know more about matter and antimatter than dark matter?

In Your Own Words

1. Which idea, theory, or space object from this book would you be most interested in learning more about? What could you do to learn more about it?

2. What is one thing you'd like to know about space that is not mentioned in this book?

3. In your opinion, which person described in the Hall of Fame sidebars did the most interesting or useful work? Why do you think so?

4. If you could go anywhere in outer space, where would you go? Why?

5. Why do you think no one has gone to the moon in the last 50 years?

Glossary

atom a tiny particle that is a building block of matter

electric current a flow of particles that carry an electric charge

electricity a form of energy caused by the flow of electrons

electron a negatively charged particle; one of the three main particles that make up an atom

energy the ability to do work that can be stored and transferred in different ways

engineer a person who designs and builds machines and structures

force a push or pull that can change the movement or shape of an object

galaxy a large group of stars held together by gravity

gravity a force of attraction between all objects that have mass

magnetism the property of some materials, such as iron, to attract or repel similar materials

magnify to make something appear larger than it is

mass the amount of matter in an object

matter something that has mass and takes up space

nebula a cloud of gas and dust in space

neutron a particle with no electric charge, found in the nucleus of most atoms

nucleus the central part of an atom, made up of protons and neutrons

orbit the circular path of a body around a more massive body

particle a tiny unit of matter

pressure the amount of force acting over an area

proton a particle with a positive charge, found in an atom's nucleus

radiation an electromagnetic wave or a stream of particles that comes from a radioactive source

refraction the change in direction of a wave when it moves from one material to another, such as when light moves through a lens

relativity a set of ideas in physics that explain how space and time are linked

subatomic smaller than an atom

vacuum an area without any matter in it

velocity a measure of how far something travels over a set period of time and in a direction

weight the measure of the gravity felt by an object with mass

Read More

Bolte, Mari. *Our Solar System (Wonders of the Webb Telescope).* Ann Arbor, MI: Cherry Lake Press, 2023.

Goldstein, Margaret J. *Mysteries of Black Holes (Space Mysteries).* Minneapolis: Lerner Publishing Group, 2021.

Isaacson, Walter. *Albert Einstein: The Man, the Genuis, and the Theory of Relativity (Pioneers of Science).* New York: Rosen Publishing, 2022.

Nardo, Don. *Reaching into the Universe: Advances in Space Exploration.* San Diego, CA: ReferencePoint Press, Inc., 2024.

Learn More Online

1. Go to **FactSurfer.com** or scan the QR code below.

2. Enter "**Space & Time**" into the search box.

3. Click on the cover of this book to see a list of websites.

Index